ENERGY HEALING USING OILS

BOOK 2

New Colour Edition

AUTHOR

CLARE WALKER

All rights reserved Clare Walker © Copyright 2020.

The contents of this book may not be reproduced, duplicated, or transmitted without direct written permission from the author. Under no circumstances will any legal responsibility or blame be held against the publisher for any reparation, damages, or monetary loss due to the information here, either directly or indirectly.

Legal Notice:

This book is copyright protected. This is only for personal use. You cannot amend, distribute, sell, use, quote or paraphrase any part of the content within this book without the consent of the author Clare Walker.

TABLE OF CONTENTS

Table of Contents 3

INTRODUCTION..5

PART ONE 6

ESSENTIAL OILS 6

CHAPTER 1 7

THE HISTORY OF ESSENTIAL OILS 7

CHAPTER 2 9

USING ESSENTIAL OILS 9

CHAPTER 3 28

ESSENTIAL OIL RECIPES.....................................28

PART TWO...33

HEALING CRYSTALS AND OILS...........................33

CHAPTER 4 34

WHAT ARE CRYSTALS?.......................................34

CHAPTER 5 52

KNOW YOUR CHAKRAS......................................52

CHAPTER 6 67

ESSENTIAL OILS AND CRYSTALS 67

Healing the Root Chakra 67

Healing the Sacral Chakra.......................................68

Healing the Solar Plexus Chakra 69

Healing the Heart Chakra 70

Healing the Throat Chakra..71

Healing the Third Eye Chakra 72

Healing the Crown Chakra..73

PART THREE *77*

HEALING WITH ACUPUNCTURE.......................................*77*

CHAPTER 7 ....*78*

UNVEILING ACUPUNCTURE *78*

PART FOUR..*82*

AYURVEDIC THERAPY *82*

CHAPTER 8 ....*83*

HEALING WITH AYURVEDA...*83*

Ayurveda and the Elements 83

The Doshas 84

The Ayurvedic Diet...88

HEALING CHAKRAS WITH ayurveda *94*

Conclusion..*99*

REFERENCES *100*

INTRODUCTION

The ancient Indian spiritual belief that has existed for over 5000 years talks about universal energy known as *Prana*. Prana is considered the source of all life. It moves and breathes life into all. In traditional Chinese belief, there is an element called *Chi*. It is known as a universal energy that makes up all matter. It has two polar forces: the yin and the yang. These forces refer to how human energy can be balanced or unbalanced. The balanced nature of universal energy promises us good health, physically, mentally, and spiritually. The imbalanced nature, on the other hand, talks about ailments and illnesses. If our energy is unbalanced, we need to find ways to heal it.

Thankfully, since the creation of the Earth, humankind has been blessed with an abundance of resources to heal ourselves and build vital energy. Essential oils are one of those natural resources. The oils are derived from live plants, each of which has a specific chemical composition that influences the scent, absorption, and effects each oil has on the body.

ENERGY HEALING USING ESSENTIAL OILS is a beginner's guide to essential oils and the benefits each oil has for healing. It includes thorough sections that describe how essential oils can be used alone or in conjunction with crystals to enhance the therapeutic vibrations that crystals radiate. In addition, I've included a list of popular carrier oils, a chart with forty essential oils, their healing capabilities, and instructions on how to apply them, as well as 11 valuable recipes to try. Finally, the last two chapters of this book examine the healing benefits of the ancient medicines acupuncture and Ayurveda.

PART ONE

ESSENTIAL OILS

CHAPTER 1

THE HISTORY OF ESSENTIAL OILS

Essential oils are extracted from plant materials by removal methods unique to each plant. Essential oils are referred to as the liquid version of the plant. The process used for extraction influences the essential oil quality, i.e., the amount of pressure and the temperature applied throughout the extraction process. The distillation of steam is the most common extraction method and dates back over 5000 years. It works by steam vaporising over the material of the plant. The volatile components of the plants mean that they can be distilled at temperatures below boiling point, allowing the oils to be easily separated. The oils then go through a condensation process to be cooled; this is when the oils can be collected.

The Egyptians were the first to consider distillation to extract essential oils from plants made from cedarwood, cloves, and cinnamon. The Egyptians used distilled oil for embalming the dead. When discovered tombs were opened in the early twentieth century, traces of these herbs were found on the corpses.

The Greeks understood both the medicinal and aromatic advantages of plants. Hippocrates, known as the father of medicine, used fumigations for aromatic and medicinal purposes. The Roman Empire used the distillation process. Instead of concentrating on extracting essential oils, they used distillation to extract aromatic floral waters.

The 11th century was significant in the distillation of essential oils, inventing a cooling pipe allowing the plant vapours and steam to cool down more efficiently than a straight pipe.

During the 14th century, when the black death killed millions, plant and herbal preparations were used to help combat this killer plague.

In the 15th century, the amount of literature available on the medicinal properties of plants and herbs increased. In this century, Paracelsus invented the word essence, a Swiss physician who focused on using plants as medicines.

In the 20th century, a French chemist known as Rene Maurice Gattefosse was interested in the aromatic use of essential oils. However, after burning his arm and accidentally dropping it in a vat filled with lavender oil, he saw the healing benefits and eventually less scarring from using this oil. After his accident, he focused on the medicinal properties of essential oils. In 1928, he was credited with coining the term aromatherapy in an article. He promoted the beneficial use of essential oils without breaking them down. He is well known for his aromatherapy books, published in French and later translated into English. Jean Vallnet, a French surgeon, wrote the book, The Practise of Aromatherapy. He also used essential oils to treat wounded soldiers during the Second World War, which proved their worth. Madame Marguerite Maury, a biochemist, practised and taught the use of essential oils for cosmetic benefits. Robert Tisserand wrote the book The Art of Aromatherapy. He educated English speaking nations on the benefits and uses of essential oils.

CHAPTER 2

USING ESSENTIAL OILS

The Universe has given us so many natural resources to heal our energy with. Essential oils have an abundance of these healing properties. In this next chapter, I will give details of the more commonly used oils, their benefits and how they can be used.

How to Apply Essential Oils

Aromatic use: Probably the most familiar method, it involves heating oils in diffusers. Have you ever walked into a spa and breathed in the scent of tea tree oils and eucalyptus? That's essential oils working aromatically. Without a diffuser, you could add a drop of oil onto a cotton ball and place it in the area where you want the scent to linger.

Topical use: Is the application of essential oils to the skin. It involves applying essential oils to the temples, around your neck, behind your ears, and the back of your wrists. (If you're using an oil never used before, always check the label before application), also, unless the label says otherwise, you will need to use a carrier oil to dilute the Essential oil you have chosen.

Internal use of oils: This involves ingesting essential oils into the body. You can do this by adding a drop of the oil to your daily water or adding it to your recipes. Again, always check the label to make sure the oil you've bought is safe to ingest.

Types of Essential Oils

There are over 90 essential oil products. I've mentioned some of the more popular ones in the next section of this chapter.

Arborvitae: It emits a woody scent, which helps to repel bugs and deal with stress. It helps to promote a healthy and glowing complexion if blended with lavender. Avoid inhaling it excessively; it can irritate the lungs, leading to irritation of the respiratory tract. Also, it is toxic when taken orally.

Basil oil: This oil is extracted from the basil plant and has several internal and topical benefits. It is anti-inflammatory and antiviral, so you can use it to help heal colds, flu and relax your muscles. It also helps to reduce stress and treat acne.

Cassia: Cassia oil is derived from the Cinnamomum cassia plant. The oil has a spicy fragrance—a little like cinnamon, but even sweeter. Cassia oil helps to warm the body, which leaves people with a feeling of tranquillity. It should not be used by pregnant women.

Cedarwood: This oil is another earthy and naturally woody-smelling oil. It works well for beauty treatment. It can help treat eczema, acne, and dandruff, and it can also help relieve coughs and arthritis. However, don't ingest cedarwood oil. If swallowed, it can lead to vomiting, nausea, and possible damage to the digestive system.

Clary sage: It blends well with lavender, ylang-ylang, and geranium; it has a musky scent. It works well for PMS when applied to the abdomen and anxiety when rubbed on soles of the feet.

Elemi: This oil is a powerful antiseptic that can protect you from all types of infections, including bacteria, fungi, and viruses. Elemi is also known for balancing and restoring properties; it's a potent anti-inflammatory that helps to boost digestion and circulation.

Frankincense: This oil has various kinds of astringent, antiseptic, digestive, and disinfectant elements. It can prevent oral issues such as toothaches, bad breath, mouth sores, and cavities. It is also said to help alleviate anxiety. Frankincense is only problematic when applied to the skin, so when using, ensure it's well diluted. Aside from this, it has no other significant side effects.

Geranium: Blends well with lavender, sandalwood, and patchouli; a carrier oil is needed when applying to skin. This oil is known for its detoxifying, regenerating properties. Add a drop to face cream to hydrate and balance the skin.

Ginger: This oil is warming and stimulating. Blends well with cinnamon and grapefruit, as with all essential oils, add to a carrier oil before applying to skin. Apply to soles of feet to boost immunity, rub on wrists to help with nausea, diffuse to balance emotions.

Grapefruit: This oil gives off a bitter but fresh scent. It's best used in your diffuser. Its proven antifungal properties can reduce harmful bacteria. However, you should avoid sun exposure if you've applied grapefruit oil topically.

Jasmine: This oil blends well with lavender, sandalwood and rose. It is known to induce feelings of splendour and joy. Diffuse or apply topically to the back of the neck to help with anxiety. Add a drop to moisturiser to help with dry and irritated skin.

Hyssop: This oil is earthy and emits a sweet scent. It is used on the skin to reduce scarring and decrease inflammation. Generally, it acts as a healing agent. However, it is not meant for pregnant women or those with a history of seizures.

Helichrysum: This oil has a scent that is like a mixture of honey and hay. It has antioxidant, antifungal, antibacterial, and anti-inflammatory c

All these Oils help to promote both internal and external health. It can help to treat athlete's foot, psoriasis, and acne. It's a safe oil with few allergic side effects. This makes it an ideal oil for anyone with sensitive skin.

Lavender: This is a popular oil with numerous benefits. It has a subtle floral scent that is known for its relaxation properties. It helps to calm the mind, making drifting off to sleep effortless. In addition to this, smelling lavender oil has proven to help alleviate headaches. It can also help with itching and swelling from bug bites.

Lemon: This oil is filled with antioxidants that help to reduce inflammation. It also boosts energy and relieves nausea. Lemon is highly photosensitive. If you are applying it to your skin, use it at night and wash it off in the morning. Avoid sunlight when you apply the oil topically.

Melaleuca: This is commonly referred to as tea tree oil. Its medicinal scent is easy to identify. It is used as an antibacterial treatment. It can also be used as an anti-inflammatory treatment oil, and it can help to treat hypersensitivity. As a result, it has helped to treat eczema and reduce allergic reactions from nickel. You should only inhale or apply Melaleuca topically. Do not ingest this oil; it could cause digestive issues, dizziness, or hives.

Myrrh: This oil has a sappy-smelling scent. It helps to heal all forms of skin issues. It does this by relieving acne and cracked skin. It is also used for the treatment of an athlete's foot. Not to be swallowed. Not for the use of a pregnant woman as it can lead to miscarriage. Use a carrier oil if applying to the skin as it can cause dermatitis. On another serious note, it can lead to lower blood pressure and irregular heartbeat.

Neroli: This oil is derived from the bitter orange tree and has citrus and floral aromas. This oil has numerous benefits, including the ability to reduce acute and chronic inflammation. Inhaling neroli oil also helps to lower blood pressure, relieve menopausal symptoms, reduce stress, and increase sex drive. In addition, it has antioxidant and antimicrobial properties, as well as the ability to repair and rejuvenate skin.

Orange: This oil is packed with vitamin C. It has several benefits for your skin when applied topically. Many beauty products use orange oil, as it helps make skin brighter, clearer, and smoother. Health benefits from the use of orange oil include pain relief and the treatment of anxiety. However, the orange essential oil has its downsides. You must dilute it properly and avoid applying it directly to your skin. If applied to your skin, it can lead to redness and swelling. Also, avoid sunlight for 12 – 18 hours after applying this oil.

Oregano: This is a well-known spiced oil. It has antiviral, antifungal, and antibacterial benefits. It helps to treat bacteria, psoriasis, and warts. Also, its antioxidant properties make it powerful enough to heal fevers and respiratory symptoms. Pregnant women and nursing

Mothers should ask their doctors before they use oregano oil.

Patchouli: This oil relieves cold, headache, and stomach upset symptoms. It relieves depression, anxiety, and stress by providing feelings of relaxation.

Peppermint: This oil has a minty herbal scent that, when inhaled, can relieve IBS symptoms. It can also help with indigestion and headaches. If you need to heal muscle pains, try applying it to your skin. It also helps to deal with certain skin issues such as sunburn, insect bites, and itchy skin. However, you should not swallow peppermint oil because it can lead to heartburn, headaches, and mouth sores.

Roman Chamomile: This oil combines a herbal aroma with a light floral scent. It has enormous potential to put the mind at ease. All you need do is inhale it through steam. It is also helpful on the skin as it heals eczema and inflammation.

Here is a safety tip: If you are allergic to daisies, ragweed, and marigolds, avoid using Roman chamomile altogether.

Rose: Inhaling the floral scent of rose helps to reduce anxiety. It has antioxidant properties that help to heal acne and achieve younger-looking skin. However, if it is used topically, it can lead to skin irritation. Use more of the carrier oil if you want to apply rose oil to your skin.

Rosemary: This oil is energising and has a flowery scent. It's a powerful antiseptic that has antibacterial and antifungal properties. Apply directly to the skin to help wounds heal faster, or it can be added to bathwater to relieve muscle aches, joint pain, and fatigue. In addition, it can be used to relieve anxiety and tension when mixed with lavender oil.

Spearmint: In terms of fragrance and advantages, this oil is like peppermint. As a result, it can be used as a substitute for peppermint. It has antifungal properties and a sweeter scent than the others. Ask your doctor before using spearmint if you're pregnant or breastfeeding.

Spikenard: This oil is not as well-known as some other essential oils, but it has been used for thousands of years. It has a woody, musty, and spicy scent and an earthy aroma reminiscent of the roots from which it is distilled. It is used to treat stress and insomnia, fight bacteria and fungal infections, reduce inflammation, and relax the mind and body.

Vetiver: The fragrance of this oil is smoky and sweet. It's used in aromatherapy to lift one's spirits and relax nerves. It also has antioxidant properties, making it beneficial to skin protection and scar healing. It also doesn't irritate the skin. As a result, it is the best topical choice for people with sensitive skin.

Ylang-Ylang: This oil has a floral scent with soft yet spicy tones. It's been used for centuries to calm the mind, boost self-esteem, and repel insects. In addition, Ylang-ylang is commonly used in cosmetics to aid in treating skin problems and promoting hair growth.

Essential oils must be diluted in a carrier oil before they are applied to your skin. As some oils are toxic when swallowed and harmful to the skin, read the instructions on the bottle label for guidance on dilution and application before use.

Carrier Oils

When applying essential oils to the body, they should be diluted with a carrier oil known as base oil. The dilution ratio is approximately 2% essential oil to 98% base oil. However, because the instructions on the label can vary, always check them before diluting. Carrier oils are made from the fatty part of a plant; some are made from nuts and may cause a skin reaction if you are allergic to them. Please, once again, read the label on the bottle before using it. Carrier oils, unlike essential oils, do not evaporate. However, they have a shelf life and cannot be used after the date specified on the label. Avoid using mineral oil or petroleum jelly as a carrier oil because they are not natural and can clog pores, preventing essential oils from being absorbed into the skin. In addition, the carrier oil you use will affect the properties, colour, and scent of the essential oil you blend it with.

I've listed seven of the most used carrier oils over the next few pages, along with a brief description of each.

Sweet Almond oil

Slight nutty smell

Medium in thickness, nourishing to the skin.

Does not leave the skin feeling greasy after application.

Cold-pressed oil.

The typical shelf life of 1-2 years.

Avocado oil

Extremely nourishing oil.

Rich in vitamins, minerals, and omega oil.

A thicker carrier oil, which can leave a greasy or waxy feel to the skin.

It's best to mix it with another carrier oil due to its thickness.

Do not store avocado oil in the fridge, as it could alter the properties of the oil.

The estimated shelf life of 12 months.

Borage seed oil

A sweet-smelling oil commonly used in aromatherapy blends and skin care formulations. Borage seed oil has a high fatty acid content and is often used for treating dry skin conditions.

Much shorter shelf-life needs using within 6 months.

Thinner oil absorbs into the skin quickly.

The skin might feel slightly oily after application.

Coconut oil

It softens the skin and can also be used on the hair and lips but avoid using it on the face because it can clog the pores.

After use, it leaves a protective film of oil on the skin.

Grapeseed oil

Derived from grapes.

Sweet fragrance.

Thin consistency, so it is easily absorbed.

Olive oil

It can be added to other carrier oils.

Olive oil can cause reactions or sensitivities on the skin.

It should be used within 1-2 years of opening.

Rosehip seed oil

Great for treating various skin conditions, specifically dry skin conditions like eczema, psoriasis, and dermatitis.

It contains high concentrations of vitamin C and vitamin E, which are both natural antioxidants, helping to repair skin damage.

Mild earthy fragrance

Because it has a light consistency, it is quickly absorbed and leaves the skin feeling nourished.

Essential Oils and Your Health

Even though there isn't much evidence to support essential oils' healing properties. I've written about the findings of human studies and laboratory experiments conducted to determine whether essential oils can improve our health or mood. According to the website medicalnewstoday.com, the results were positive.

Anxiety and stress

Essential oils have been proven helpful in dealing with anxiety and stress. It's estimated that over 43% of people suffering from stress and anxiety have used various alternative therapies to help relieve symptoms. In this regard, aromatherapy yields positive results. When applied during massage, essential oils penetrate deeper into the skin to relieve stress and help relax tension in the muscles.

In September 2019, the article "What Are Essential Oils, and Do They Work?" was published and can be viewed online at www.healthline.com. The documented evidence that follows is from Pubmedcentral.com, a trusted source and highly respected database from the National Institute of Health.

Migraines and Headaches

There's also documented evidence from two studies that were conducted discovering that applying a mixture of peppermint oil and ethanol to a person's forehead and temples can relieve the pain of a headache. A newer study has also proven that the application of peppermint and lavender oil to the forehead can reduce headache pain. Following the traditional Persian headache remedy, applying a mixture of sesame oil and chamomile to the temples may also help treat migraines and headaches.

Sleep and Insomnia'

Lavender essential oil serves as a mild sedative and encourages deep sleep. According to a 2005 report published in the journal Chronobiology International. 31 healthy sleepers spent three nights in a sleep lab: one to adapt to the study, the second with lavender oil sprayed into the air, and the third with distilled water as a control stimulus. In both men and women, the percentage of deep and slow-wave sleep had increased. It increased sleep-in stage 2 (light). Reduced REM (rapid eye movement) sleep.

Furthermore, the morning after the lavender exposure, all the participants showed increased vigour. The fragrance of lavender oil has been shown to improve the quality of sleep among women after childbirth, according to a study approved and funded by the Tehran University of Medical Sciences in 2015. Up to fifteen studies on essential oils and sleep patterns were reviewed in one study. Most of these studies found that inhaling essential oils, especially lavender oil, improves sleep quality. Women who inhaled lavender oil slept longer and reported feeling more rested than normal.

Inflammation

According to an article published on the website sciencedirect.com, studies have shown that essential oils have anti-inflammatory effects. Could this mean that they might be effective in treating certain inflammatory conditions? Recently, a study on mice found that the ingestion of a combination of oregano essential oils and thyme helped to induce colitis remission. However, the effects of essential oils on inflammatory diseases have not been extensively studied in humans.

Antimicrobial and Antibiotic

Because of the rise of antibiotic-resistant bacteria, the scientific community is facing an increasing need to find compounds that can fight bacterial infections. Of the research done into the effectiveness of essential oils for these purposes, using oils such as tea tree and peppermint had positive results.

On the following five pages, I've included a chart that can be used as a reference when creating your own remedies with essential oils.

PROBLEM	ESSENTIAL OIL	HOW TO USE
Indigestion Flatulence Muscle spasm	Aniseed	Massage onto stomach
Coughs Indigestion Fever	Basil	Inhalation Bath Massage
Respiration Indigestion Rheumatism	Bay	Inhalation Bath Massage
Irritated skin Throat infections	Benzoin	Inhalation Massage
Fatigue	Bergamot	Inhalation Bath
Muscle spasm	Black pepper	Massage
Respiratory Digestive problems	Cajeput	Inhalation Bath Massage
Dry skin Mental fatigue Eczema Acne	Cedarwood	Massage Inhalation Skincare
Inflammation	Chamomile	Inhalation

		Bath
		Massage
		Compress
Nausea Digestive problems	Cinnamon	Massage
Insect repellent Hard skin	Citronella	Vaporisation Skin care
Stress Hormonal problems Muscle aches	Clary Sage	Inhalation Compress Bath Creams
Skin infections	Clove	Massage
Oily skin	Cypress	Massage
Decongestant Antiseptic	Eucalyptus	Inhalation Compress Bath Creams
Constipation Menstrual pain	Fennel	Inhalation Massage
Inflammation Mental fatigue	Frankincense	Inhalation Bath
Irritated skin	Geranium	Bath Cream
Muscle aches	Ginger	Inhalation

Fatigue Stomach upsets		Compress
Anxiety Fatigue Depression	Grapefruit	Inhalation Bath
Stress	Jasmine	Inhalation Bath Massage
Dry skin Acne Balancing Relaxing	Lavender	Inhalation Compress Bath
Respiration Fatigue Circulation Toning	Lemon	Inhalation Massage
Muscle aches Infections Stress	Lemongrass	Massage Bath
Stress Insomnia Muscle spasms	Marjoram	Inhalation Compress Bath
Respiration	Melissa	Bath

Stress Hormonal disorders		
Respiratory Menstrual disorders	Myrrh	Inhalation Skincare
Stress Digestive upsets Dry skin	Neroli	Inhalation Massage Compress Bath
Respiratory Energy boost Oily skin	Orange	Massage Bath Skincare
Damaged skin Mental fatigue Aphrodisiac	Patchouli	Skincare Massage
Digestive disorders Fatigue Soothing sore feet	Peppermint	Inhalation Creams Compress Bath
Anxiety Insomnia Skincare	Petitgrain	Inhalation Skincare
Damaged skin Fatigue	Pine	Massage Inhalation

Muscle aches		
Dry, mature skin Menstrual disorders	Rose	Inhalation Cream Bath
Dry, sensitive skin	Rose Otto	Inhalation Massage Cream Bath Skincare
Pain relief Digestion Dandruff Stress	Rosemary	Inhalation Creams Compress Bath
Fever Appetite Stimulant Joint pain	Sage	Inhalation Massage
Respiratory Fungal infections Skin infections	Tea tree	Inhalation Compress Bath
Appetite Energy boost Infections	Sweet Thyme	Bath Inhalation

Stress	Ylang-ylang	Inhalation
Depression		Cream
Long hair		Bath
		Massage

CHAPTER 3

ESSENTIAL OIL RECIPES

Allergies

A rub for pollen, dust, and pet hair allergies.

6 drops of lavender.

6 drops of chamomile.

2 drops of myrrh.

1 drop of peppermint.

30ml carrier oil.

Blend the mixture together.

Apply to behind the ears and the temples.

Boost energy

15 drops of peppermint.

20 drops of orange.

15 ml of carrier oil.

It's best to place this mix in a small jar and carry it around with you.

When you feel like your energy is low, place some on the back of the neck, on the temples and inhale.

Detox body scrub

2 cups of brown sugar.

1 cup of carrier oil.

4 drops of orange.

4 drops of basil.

4 drops of lemon.

4 drops of rosemary.

4 drops of grapefruit.

4 drops of lavender.

Mix the ingredients and place them in a storage tub-preferably glass.

Use weekly to exfoliate and assist in the elimination of toxins.

Hair growth booster

5 drops cedarwood.

5 drops of cypress.

5 drops of lavender.

5 drops of rosemary oil.

2 tablespoons of coconut oil.

Shower cap or towel.

Mix ingredients together and massage into the scalp. Wear a shower cap or wrap your hair in a towel.

Leave on the hair for a few hours or overnight, then shampoo and condition.

Strong Nails

2 drops of lemon.

2 drops of frankincense.

2 drops of myrrh.

10 ml of carrier oil.

Mix ingredients together and massage into the cuticles. Re-apply twice weekly.

Headache Soother

7 drops of peppermint.

 5 drops of lavender.

5 drops of frankincense.

5ml of carrier oil.

Apply to the temples and back of the neck and re-apply every 30 minutes or as needed.

Mental Fatigue

1 drop of cedarwood.

1 drop of frankincense.

1 drop of patchouli.

1 drop of sandalwood.

10 ml of carrier oil.

Once mixed, place on the back of the neck whenever you feel mental fatigue or need a boost of energy.

Muscle bath soak

3 drops of lavender.

2 drops of chamomile.

1 cup of Epsom salts.

Add the oils to the Epsom salts before adding to the bath, allowing the oils to better dissolve. For best results, soak in the bath for a minimum of 20 minutes.

Lavender bath soak

Castile soap 250gram.

A cup of hot water.

30 drops of essential lavender oil.

20 drops of chamomile oil.

A 500 ml bottle

A container (large enough to mix the solution).

A funnel

A knife.

Cut the soap into cubes around 1 inch in size, place in the container, cover with the hot water and mix well. When the soap has melted, use the funnel to pour the mixture into the bottle. Add the oil to the mixture. Seal the bottle and shake well. Always store the oil in a cool place, shielded from direct light and shake before each use.

Soothing sleep rub

¼cup of coconut oil

¼cup of cocoa butter

20 drops of lavender

6 drops of cedarwood.

6 drops of Ylang-ylang

10 drops of frankincense

Warm the coconut oil and cocoa butter, allow cooling before mixing with the essential oils. Massage a small amount into the feet before bed.

Sunburn soother

25 drops of lavender.

25 drops of peppermint.

10 ml of carrier oil.

When mixing this, a good choice of carrier oil would be avocado. It is high in antioxidants and omegas to replace those lost by the Sun, helping repair the skin quickly.

PART TWO

HEALING CRYSTALS AND OILS

CHAPTER 4

WHAT ARE CRYSTALS?

Crystals are powerful stones that have been studied and used by humankind for thousands of years. There is incredible healing power embedded in these natural elements, which I will explain in the next part of this book.

Crystals: Healing and Humanity

Tracing the history of humanity with crystals, you will find that crystals have been used throughout time as a means and source of healing power. Crystals were well known by the Egyptians, Sumerians, and Mayans. They showed their understanding of crystals by adorning themselves, their jewellery, and homes with these sacred stones. Yet, despite the predominance of crystal knowledge among these cultures, our modern world has not fully harnessed the effective power that lies in the stones.

In my last book, "Energy Healing Using Crystals", I told of the people of Big Bear Valley who needed nature to smile on them again; they desperately needed rain. The valley had experienced a decade of dryness and poor crop growth. Animals were emigrating, and the plants were withering and dying. There was an urgent need for the people to find a solution to the problem. During a meeting among the people, a crazy idea was proposed. There was a legend that the people who once lived on that land knew how to heal it and that one of them, a Shaman knew as Blue Thunder, still had that ancient wisdom. It all seemed a little desperate and farfetched but feeling as though they had no other option, they called him and asked for help.

Blue Thunder came and explained how everything is connected to Mother Earth through ley lines (where Earth's natural energy vibrates). Unfortunately, the ley lines that ran through the valley were disrupted by men building roads and pollution. He said the valley was suffering because of this but, with the use of crystals and prayer, he could heal the ley lines and bring water back to the land.

His healing method was to identify the energy lines in the valley which were broken and place crystals in these certain areas to create a free space where the energy was blocked to promote healing. He had what seems to be a mysterious crow that was busy cleaning the negative energy around him as he proceeded on healing the energy of the land with crystals. It soon became apparent his actions were successful because the much-needed rain soon came, followed by snow. The volcano that had started to show signs of activity was once again dormant. His actions healed the valley, bringing animals and plant life back once more.

The story of "Big Bear Valley" seems to be a legend. Yet, it's a true story, and the documented evidence is available to watch. You will find more amazing facts about the Shamon Blue Thunder and the valley he healed if you check my first book. I have repeated a part of the story to show an example of crystals and their healing abilities.

Crystals are powerful and possess the ability to receive and direct healing energy to all that they surround.

There are different types of crystals, each having its own vibrational frequency. And, each has its own specific healing powers, whether it be the mind, the body, or the soul. The use of crystals helps to promote a good flow of energy, as negative energy is being cleansed from the body. They can also be used to clean negative energy from the air when placed in rooms.

For decades, scientists assumed that the atom was constructed from particles (protons, electrons, and neutrons). We now know them to be packets of energy. This means to put in layman's terms that basically, every living thing on Earth has an energy vibration, crystals have the highest. The beauty of them is they can raise the energy vibration of anything around them.

Scientists have successfully found a use for the energy in small quartz crystals by using it to keep time in the watches we use and the electronic components in smartphones and computers. Modern technology understands the energetic properties of healing crystals. It has not failed to use them to the fullest of its possibilities. Medication is filled with crystals. Most pharmaceutical manufacturers make their drugs by grinding them up, adding to the ingredients. Despite all these applications of the energetic properties of crystals, many people are yet to understand their energetic healing benefits. Crystal healing works with energy in the same way that magnets use energy to repel and attract. When you place a crystal on your body, you'll experience a transformation of your energy: your vibration will be raised based on the properties and energetic signature of the crystal.

Crystals heal: No boundaries or limitations exist to healing the body, mind, and soul with the right crystals. They help to heal anxiety, migraines, sadness, and more.

Crystals cleanse: You can cleanse energy with the help of crystals, having the capacity to absorb negative energy from a person's body that doesn't belong there, just like a magnet picking up a piece of metal. Clear quartz is great for removing negative energy. It can be used for cleansing the energy in a room, at home, or wherever you may be. Just remember, because of the amount of negative energy they absorb, Clear crystals need to be cleaned more often than others to keep them charged with high vibrational energy.

Crystals energise: Are you suffering from fatigue or feeling run down and in need of a boost in energy? If so, choose a yellow crystal. Sunstone is good for healing chronic fatigue, helping you to regain vitality.

Crystal's balance: Everything we know is connected by vibrational energy; these vibrations seem to hold the Universe together. If our energy changes suddenly, it can cause our vibrations to resonate at a lower frequency, which can cause a lot of problems, even illness. However, crystals have their own vibrational energy. They can transfer to our bodies, increase our energy vibrations, and balance our chakras, thus restoring health once more.

Types of Crystals

In the following section, I have categorised crystals based on their colours and their healing benefits.

The Brown: Protection and Grounding

Petrified Wood, Tiger's Eye, Halite

(IMAGE: TIGER'S EYE)

Crystals in the brown category are grounding. Brown crystals are like a dirt path in the dark woods: they protect you on your journey. Brown crystals serve as guides and protectors. They clear the way for us. You might find them useful when you need something new in your life, such as a new relationship.

The Red: Action and Power

Garnet, Ruby, Jasper

(IMAGE: RED JASPER)

The crystals in the red category stimulate your root chakra are great for giving your energy a boost. They can improve fertility and sex drive, ease period pain, blood disorders, frigidity and increase courage. If you need the motivation to engage in something, carry a red crystal with you.

The White/Clear: Purity and Peace

Moonstone, Quartz, Selenite

(Image: Moonstone)

White crystals stimulate the Crown Chakra and increase your general well being. These stones are absorbent and help to clear negative energy. Many people use crystal quartz while meditating because it helps to clear and calm the mind. White crystals also improve self-esteem and depression. However, the crown chakra should not have too much direct stimulus, so place your crystal under your pillow while sleeping at night.

Violet: Spirituality and Intuition

Iolite, Amethyst, Sugilite, Labradorite, Flourite

(Image: Iolite)

The crystals in the violet category stimulate the third eye chakra, boost concentration and mental awareness. Their vibration is what makes these stones some of the most powerful. They have a high vibrational frequency, placing them at the top of our colour spectrum. Violet crystals connect you to a higher plane of existence. If you want to be uplifted, if you want to induce a spiritual experience, or if you need higher powers to be your guide, violet crystals are the answer.

Orange Crystals: *Change and Creativity*

Aragonite, Citrine, Copper, Sunstone

(Image: Sunstone)

The Sacral chakra is responsible for our creativity and sexuality. It is stimulated by orange crystals. Do you ever get that feeling when you're outside in the sunshine, and all your troubles seem to fade away? It's because the colour orange soothes and energises our body, mind, and spirit. Orange crystals flush out negative energy, making way for positive energy to resonate in the body.

Green: Abundance and Growth

Malachite, Emerald, Jade

(Image: Jade)

The heart chakra is balanced by green and pink crystals. Stress and depression will result if the energy in this Chakra is out of sync. Green crystals attract abundance, wealth, increase self-esteem and cultivate happiness. They have balancing properties and increase affection, compassion, and empathy in the Heart. Green crystals encourage you to keep working even though things are difficult. Carrying a green crystal with you will make you feel content, optimistic, and more mindful of your own beauty.

Blue: Clarity and Communication

Angelite, Sapphire, Sodalite

(Image: Sodalite)

The throat chakra is balanced by blue crystals. On the mind, they have a soothing and stimulating effect. They help people improve their communication skills and self-expression. All you need are blue crystals to hear or discover the truth about something. They relieve anxiety and ear, nose, and throat problems by allowing you to express yourself while remaining calm and collected.

Yellow: Optimism and Willpower

Citrine, Amber, Mookaite

(Image: Amber)

Yellow crystals stimulate the solar plexus chakra. If you have an unhealthy habit you need to break? or you are trying to build a new, healthier habit? Yellow stones cleanse and reorganise your energy patterns.

Indigo: Spiritual journeys

Lapis Lazuli, Azurite, Kyanite

(Image: Lapis Lazuli)

Indigo crystals stimulate the third eye chakra. Our lives won't always be filled with calmness and joy. There are times when chaos will reign. In these moments, you need calmness. This is where the soothing power of indigo or dark blue healing stones comes to play. Address anxiety, self-esteem and fragile energy with any of the stones in his category.

Black: Negativity Blockers

Apache Tears, Tourmaline, Obsidian

(Image: Black Tourmaline)

Do you need refuge or protection? Black crystals are there for you. They deflect negativity; they are strong and resilient, making them protective. You can use them to repel any form of negative energy, reducing fear and anxiety along with increasing your critical thinking ability.

Pink: Love and Compassion

Rhodonite, Rose Quartz, Morganite

(Image: Rhodonite)

Pink stones are connected with the heart chakra, which is located in the centre of the chest. They are referred to as the "love stones." They can help to protect and restore relationships, even help you to attract love. They can help with emotional issues such as stress, rage, and sadness and alleviate heart and chest problems. When you see pink, you think of romance. The reason is simple, pink crystals have compassionate vibrations; they have love energy. They help you address anger by deflecting it, helping you to feel loved, raising self-esteem and restoring confidence.

Using Healing Crystals

Placing them on the body: If you need healing in a specific location (as mentioned, the colour of the crystal is key to its healing quality). Place the crystal directly on the part of your body that needs it. For example, you can sit and place a Fluorite crystal on your head to help ease the pain if you have a headache or Amber if suffering from a migraine.

Wearing them: Some crystals are best worn on the body; they help keep your energy vibrations balanced throughout the day. Sometimes, however, it's hard to wear a stone where it is needed. For instance, if the problem was your eye and you were staying in, you could wear a crystal on your Third Eye Chakra. However, if you were going out, as a second choice, you could wear the crystal on your Heart Chakra as all chakras are linked. It will send the energy to where it's required; it doesn't need to be directly placed on the problem area.

Crystal grid: Involves creating a specific predetermined pattern with a certain type of crystal. The patterns are created to receive and send energy. This method is ancient and may take time to learn. However, it's worth it, as it can be a powerful practice.

Meditation: You can use crystals as you meditate. Crystal healing is millions of years ahead of us, and they hold a whole lot of information dating back to times we don't even know. Suppose you sit with crystals whilst calming your mind during meditation. In that case, you will increase your sensitivity to receiving life-changing and amazing insights.

Sleeping near them: When you sleep, your subconscious mind is at work. This is the best time to be healed and to learn fast. Placing crystal stones around you when you sleep will eradicate every hurdle in your conscious mind, so you can easily deal with fear and doubt. You should try placing a clear quartz crystal under your pillow or on your bedside table. You will still benefit from its healing vibration as you sleep and feel calmer when you wake in the morning.

Crystals on your body: You don't need to leave crystals in a particular place for them to work their magic. It's even better to move the stones all around you to experience powerful and accelerated healing. For example, to clear negative energy, try moving a crystal from your head to your toes. The human energy field extends up to three feet around us, so don't hesitate to work on your whole aura while you engage in crystal healing.

Welcome crystals in your home and car: Placing crystals in your car and home can protect you from undesirable events. You can block negative energy by wearing crystals, or placing them in your home, respectively.

Cleansing your Crystals

You must clean your crystals regularly to wash away the negative energy they've absorbed. You should clean your crystal as soon as you take it home after buying it because the crystal could have sat weeks before it came to you, absorbing the energy from around it and from anyone who touched it. This can cause the crystal's energy to vibrate at a low frequency, leaving it unbalanced. Then the crystal can be charged with your energy.

Soak your crystal in purified water, holy water, or saltwater (you should not do this to Amber or selenite because they are likely to dissolve). You can also perform smudging, which involves using the smoke from white sage, incense, or a joss stick to cleanse your crystals. Some people give their crystals a moon bath. This involves placing the crystals out at night under the full moonlight. It is also possible to charge your crystals by holding them in your hands. Close your eyes and hold the crystal in the palm of your right hand. Consider a beam of white light entering your body through your crown chakra. Imagine this white light flooding the body with soothing energy and driving any harmful energy out with each breath. Once you've filled yourself with white light. Imagine yourself sharing the white healing light with the crystal, stating your reason for purchasing it, and thanking it for the healing you will receive. When you need energy healing from crystals, hold them in your left hand.

Crystals are powerful healing tools with a long history. If they were helpful in the ages that are no more, they are still efficient in today's times. So start harnessing the power of crystals to break free from all forms of negative energy and build strong positive vibrations and energy around yourself.

CHAPTER 5

KNOW YOUR CHAKRAS

As humans, we need a consistent flow of energy through our bodies. The consistency in this flow has a lot to do with how our body, mind, and soul are connected to form a wholeness. In "Energy Healing Using Crystals", I mentioned our chakras and how they can be healed with crystals. In this guide, I've explained a little more about chakras and given a description of each, along with explaining how to balance each of the chakras using crystals and essential oils.

The word "chakra" means "wheel." It is a term used in Sanskrit to describe the flow of energy in the human body. There are seven chakras in the body; they are our energy centres. Chakras originate from Buddhism and Hinduism. Following meditation practice, if any chakra becomes out of balance, it will have a negative impact on your physical, mental, and spiritual health. Every Chakra is linked to a specific part of the body and serves a specific purpose. I've mentioned each of the seven chakras, as well as the crystals that work best with each one, in the following section of this chapter.

Let's now look at these seven chakras.

The Root Chakra / The Muladhara

This is the first Chakra in the human body. It is found at the base of the spine. The root chakra connects the mind, body, and soul to the Earth, providing a sense of security, stability, grounding necessary to benefit from all the Earth's resources. First, imagine deep roots emerging inside of you and out through the soles of your feet as an effortless way of connecting to the Earth and grounding yourself. Then, imagine the roots reaching all the way to the Earth's core, where they absorb the Universe's unconditional love, support, and understanding.

If the root chakra is balanced, you will have a positive outlook on life, be grounded, present in the moment, optimistic without being arrogant, and be passionate about your desires without allowing your Heart to rule your head.

If your root chakra is blocked, you may experience a run of bad luck, failure, feelings of unworthiness, lack of trust, and exhaustion.

Essential oil to balance the root chakra: Patchouli.

Crystals to balance the root chakra: Garnet, Ruby, Tourmaline, Obsidian, and Bloodstone.

Affirmations: "I am grounded", I am safe."

Tones: 128 hertz, 256 hertz, and 512 hertz are ideal for the root chakra.

Element: Earth.

Colour: Red.

The Sacral Chakra / The Svadhisthana

Located just below the navel, the Sacral Chakra governs creativity, emotions, and sexual desires. If balanced, you will have a positive outlook on life, appreciate challenges, and be aware of your own strengths and weaknesses. As a result, you'll want to try new things, have positive relationships without letting your ego get in the way of your goals.

If this chakra is blocked, you could be emotionally and physically exhausted. It can also cause addictions, fear OF change, sexual dysfunction, and lack of motivation.

Crystals to balance the Sacral Chakra: Amber, Carnelian, and Jasper.

Essential oils to balance the Sacral Chakra: Ylang-ylang, Orange, and Jasmine.

Affirmations: "At my core, I am joy; I welcome joy to flow into my life." "It is good to feel my emotions; I am safe. This is how I honour myself."

Tones: 144hertz, 288 hertz, and 576 hertz are ideal for balancing the Sacral Chakra.

Element: Water

Colour: Orange.

The Solar Plexus Chakra / The Manipura

The solar plexus chakra is located at the top of the abdomen, in the space between the rib cages. It is the Chakra that aligns us to our own personal power. It promotes happiness and positivity, as well as self-control, self-confidence, and wisdom. Our "gut feeling" is also managed by the solar plexus chakra.

If the solar plexus chakra is balanced, you will have an air of confidence, realising and accepting the positive meaning of life. You will be able to look forward to all the good things that life may bring your way.

If this Chakra is blocked, You may feel demotivated, insecure, or tend to be a people-pleaser. You might believe that you need to gain acceptance from others to be satisfied with your decisions and accomplishments.

The solar plexus chakra is yellow.

Essential oil to balance the solar plexus chakra: Black Pepper and Grapefruit.

Crystals to balance the solar plexus chakra: Yellow Calcite and Citrine.

Tones: 126 hertz, 324 hertz, and 648 hertz are ideal for balancing the solar plexus chakra.

Affirmations: "I am safe, powerful, and in control."

Element: Fire

The Heart Chakra / The Anahata

The heart chakra, located in the centre of the chest, is our fourth energy centre. It's seen as the core of our human experience because it determines our compassion and level of trust, which influences how we allow ourselves to love and be loved.

If the heart chakra is balanced, it will radiate love, attracting positive influences into your life, along with strengthening existing relationships. You will have a passion for living and want the best for everybody around you. It will bring you joy to see people you know doing well.

If the heart chakra is blocked, life may appear unfair, and you may perceive yourself to have little or no potential. You may say you don't want or need love from others but will secretly crave closeness just like the rest of us. You may feel isolated from everything and everyone, and you may be extremely shy.

The heart chakra is green.

Tone frequencies of 182.25 hertz, 364.5 hertz, and 792 hertz are beneficial for balancing the heart chakra.

Essential oil: Rose oil

Crystals: Green aventurine and Rose quartz

Element: Air

Affirmation: "It is safe for me to love and be loved."

The Throat Chakra / The Vishuddha

Located in the throat, this is the 5th energy centre of the 7 main chakras. It is what gives us a voice in society. It works with our creativity, clear and effective communication, self-expression, and speaking the truth.

There are numerous advantages to having a balanced throat Chakra. There will be positivity radiating from within you, allowing you to speak your truth with great confidence. This includes your demeanour, words, the songs you sing, the tunes you hum, and the melodies you whistle.

You may find it tough to express yourself or believe that what you're trying to say isn't getting across. Writer's block and issues finishing a school project or perhaps a report that needs to be handed in can all be signs of a blocked throat Chakra. Panic attacks, claustrophobic feelings, and anxiousness can all be physical indications of a blocked throat Chakra. Neck pain is also a possibility.

The throat chakra is blue.

Tones: 192 hertz, 384 hertz, and 768 hertz are good for balancing the throat Chakra.

Element: Sound

Essential oils: Lemon, Peppermint, German chamomile, and Frankincense.

Crystals: Turquoise, Aquamarine, and Kyanite.

Affirmation: "I speak my heart's truth with confidence."

The Third Eye Chakra / The Ajna

The third eye chakra is translated to mean "beyond wisdom." It's located on the forehead in-between the eyebrows, associated with intuition, the wisdom of the higher self and creative inspiration, as it opens the door to inner wisdom.

When the third eye is balanced, you'll be connected to the Divine, your spirit guides, and angels; and open to all that the Universe has to offer. Furthermore, a healthy third eye chakra allows you to have strong intuition and pick up on signs and signals from the Universe. It also has much to do with imagination and allowing you to see the big picture in life.

If the third eye chakra is blocked, you may question your life's purpose and believe that everything you do is insignificant. It may also be difficult for you to make decisions. Physically, you may have trouble sleeping and lack concentration. It's also possible to suffer from headaches, back pain, and leg pain when this Chakra is blocked.

The third eye chakra is indigo.

Tones: 216 hertz, 432 hertz, and 864 hertz are good for balancing the third eye chakra.

Essential oils: Sandalwood, Clary sage, and Lemon.

Crystals: Labradorite, Amethyst, and Lapis lazuli.

Element: Ether

Affirmations: "I am life, and life is me." "I am one with the Universe."

The Crown Chakra / The Sahasrara

Our seventh energy centre is the crown chakra. It can be found in the crown area of the head. This Chakra is, in a sense, the portal to the Universe. The third eye establishes a connection with the Divine, which can be maintained through the crown chakra.

If the crown chakra is balanced, you will have a steady energy flow, universal consciousness and receive clear communication from the Devine. Your thoughts and emotions form the vibration you send out into the

Universe as communication; you will gain insight into yourself, along with having enlightenment and transcendence.

If your crown chakra is blocked, you may feel disconnected from life. You may struggle to find joy in insignificant things, lack motivation, and feel disconnected from your spirituality. Physically, you may experience migraines, poor coordination, and constant fatigue.

The crown chakra is violet.

Tones: 243 hertz, 486 hertz, and 972 hertz are good for balancing the crown chakra.

Essential oils: Lime, Rose, Cedarwood, and Helichrysum.

Element: Thought

Crystals: Amethyst, Moonstone, Flourite, and Clear quartz.

Affirmations: "I honour the Divine within me." "I am guided by a higher power and inner wisdom."

CHAPTER 6

ESSENTIAL OILS AND CRYSTALS

As stated previously, the body has seven chakras from the base of the spine to the crown of the head. They are our energy centres, absorbing energy from the environment and the people around them. They are our energetic connection to the Universe, keeping the body balanced and our emotions in check. If the chakras are blocked or unbalanced, it can negatively impact the entire body, affecting physical, mental, and spiritual health.

In this chapter, I'd like to discuss how combining crystals and essential oils can balance the chakras.

Healing the Root Chakra

As previously stated, the root chakra is the centre of our basic needs; it gives us a sense of grounding and connects the mind, body, and spirit to the energy of the Earth. When this Chakra is balanced, you will feel calm and secure. You will have the ability to tackle new challenges or a life change, like a new job, new relationship, or a moving house, with ease and confidence.

Negative thoughts, disconnectedness, anxiety, and insecurity can all be symptoms of a blocked or unbalanced root chakra. The colour red suggests that the root chakra is warm, protective, and fierce. As a result, choosing a crystal from the same colour family is recommended. Red and black crystals are known for their grounding properties and thus work well with the root chakra. Go-to crystals include Ruby, Garnet, Obsidian, Red Jasper and Black Tourmaline. Patchouli essential oil is good for root chakra balancing because it helps heal feelings of separation and isolation. It provides you with a sense of security, peace, and grounding.

Healing the Sacral Chakra

The Sacral chakra is associated with our emotions, sexuality, creativity, and ability to adapt to change. When this Chakra is balanced, you will have a positive outlook on life, even if you are going through tough times or have challenges ahead of you. You will be enjoyable to be around, welcome challenges, and your attitude towardS them will be one from which everyone benefits.

Because the sacral chakra deals with emotions, when blocked, it is extremely difficult to control them. Furthermore, this Chakra is so important to your sense of identity and sexuality. If it's blocked, it's likely to cause relationship issues, excessive shyness, boredom, being uninspired, or a fear of intimacy.

Because the Sacral Chakra is associated with the colour orange, crystals like Amber, Jasper, and Carnelian complement it well. These crystals are well-known for their ability to reduce the negative effects of emotional burdens and protect against negative energies such as envy, rage, hatred, and fear. By calming and balancing your emotions, they help you express yourself, bringing positivity into your life.

Choose calming oils like Jasmine, Ylang-ylang, and Orange, which have similar beneficial properties to the crystals mentioned above and enhance their healing vibration when used together.

Healing the Solar Plexus Chakra

This Chakra is regarded as the centre of the body. It possesses all emotions, stresses, and the body's nerve centre. It oversees making you feel in control, motivating you, and developing your self-esteem. When balanced, you will feel in control of your life, independent, and capable of accomplishing anything you set your mind to. However, suppose the solar plexus chakra is unbalanced. In that case, you may begin to feel egoistic, insecure, have low self-esteem, and lack confidence.

Because the solar plexus chakra is yellow and uses the Sun's energy, Yellow Calcite and Citrine crystals are excellent choices for healing it. These crystals are well-known for amplifying energy, transforming ideas into action, and providing innovative solutions to problems that benefit all parties involved. Use essential oils that are restorative and balancing to complement these crystals.

Black pepper is beneficial to the solar plexus chakra because it helps to transform rigid patterns and mental concepts. It teaches you that you don't have to repeat past mistakes and allows you to see fresh solutions to old problems.

Grapefruit oil is also a good option because of its refreshing and uplifting scent, which helps relieve depression and anxiety. Combined with Citrine, it brings joy and creativity back into our lives, builds good self-esteem, and attracts abundance while balancing the solar plexus chakra.

Healing the Heart Chakra

Our fourth energy centre, the heart chakra, is associated with the colour green. Our level of trust is determined by the heart chakra, which influences how we allow ourselves to love and be loved. The heart chakra is regarded as the centre of our human experience and is associated with Universal love.

When your Heart Chakra is balanced, you will be at peace and compassionate during challenging times. In addition, you will have a powerful desire to do what is best for yourself and those around you.

When the heart chakra becomes blocked, jealousy and a fear of love may emerge. You may believe you have little or no potential and that you are significantly different from others. Even when surrounded by people, you may feel constant, heartbreaking loneliness.

This Chakra is green, but it is linked to the compassionate power of pink. Rose quartz and green aventurine crystals are effective for heart chakra healing. These crystals provide relief from heartache and past traumas. They assist you in experiencing life to the fullest by shifting your focus from the mind to the Heart.

Rose oil is a great option for balancing the heart chakra. It encourages self-acceptance, compassion, and a desire to work from the Heart toward enlightenment.

Healing the Throat Chakra

The throat chakra is represented by the colour blue and is the fifth energy centre of the seven major chakras. Affecting your ability to listen, communicate, be confident, express yourself, and love.

Having a healthy throat chakra has numerous benefits. Firstly, it helps you communicate with tenderness and reliability while allowing you to state your truth confidently through your body language and words.

When the throat chakra is blocked, you may feel tongue-tied or use harsh words. It can cause nervousness, anxiety, panic attacks, and persistent fear.

The throat chakra is associated with the colour blue. Aquamarine, kyanite, and turquoise are beneficial crystals for balancing it; they help you find acceptance, peace, and relief from symptoms of anything that affects the body negatively. They also aid in the elimination of toxic patterns.

For balancing the throat chakra, I highly recommend Frankincense essential oil. This oil heightens spiritual awareness, deepening your connection to the Divine. In addition, it encourages clear, effective communication, discouraging reactivity, allowing you to respond gracefully to any situation. Essential oils such as lemon, peppermint, and German chamomile are also beneficial to the throat chakra.

Healing the Third Eye Chakra

The sixth energy centre in the body is the third eye chakra, often known as the seat of the soul. It's located on the forehead, in the area between the eyes. This Chakra governs your psychic capacity; it is the gateway to your inner realms, higher consciousness, and imagination.

When this Chakra is balanced, you will communicate clearly with the Universe and be receptive to all the knowledge it has to offer. As a result, you will feel forgiveness, tranquillity, and a sense of purpose in your life.

When the third eye chakra is blocked, life can feel overwhelming; you may begin to distrust your inner voice and lose access to intuition.

Because the third eye chakra is indigo in colour. The go-to crystals for balancing this energy centre include Labradorite, Amethyst, and lapis lazuli crystals. These crystals are ideal for establishing a deep and clear connection with the Universe, averting negative energy and offering a sense of spirituality, happiness, and peace.

Use an essential oil associated with clarity and wisdom, such as sandalwood. This oil provides a sense of peace when engaging with higher consciousness and inner awareness. It supports alignment with your most genuine self, the dissolving of illusions, and the improvement of meditation, spiritual practice, and healing.

Healing the Crown Chakra

The crown chakra, often known as "the gateway to the cosmos," is the 7th of the body's main energy centres. It's violet in colour and situated in the crown area, above the head. It connects us to the Divine, and it has a unique role in spirituality, enlightenment, and universal consciousness. When we activate this Chakra, we feel connected to the cosmos and our higher self.

When the crown chakra is blocked, you may experience disconnection from life, negativity, and loneliness. As a result, you may struggle with meditation, feel restless, and prefer to be alone.

The crown chakra can be balanced using white/clear and violet crystals such as Clear

Quartz, Amethyst and Moonstone. The Clear quartz crystal is particularly beneficial for crown chakra work. It balances the entire physical body, including boosting the immune system. It raises your vibration, which enhances your natural psychic ability allowing clear communication with the infinite wisdom of the Universe. However, all these crystals are powerful and can draw positive energy from the Universe into your life. They relieve anxiety and stress, allowing you to relax sufficiently to the level required to initiate a profound spiritual connection.

Select essential oils that encourage detachment from the physical world and support connection with the Divine. These include Lavender, Lime, Cedarwood, Helichrysum, and Rose oil.

The Balancing Table

Chakras	Crystals	Essential oils
The Root Chakra	Black Tourmaline Garnet Bloodstone Obsidian Red-Jasper Ruby	Patchouli Vetiver Cypress
The Sacral Chakra	Amber Jasper Carnelian	Orange Jasmine Ylang-Ylang
The Solar Plexus Chakra	Yellow Calcite Citrine	Grapefruit Black Pepper
The Heart Chakra	Aventurine Rose quartz	Rose
The Throat Chakra	Kyanite Aquamarine Turquoise	Lemon Peppermint German Chamomile Frankincense

The Third Eye Chakra	Labradorite Lapis-lazuli Amethyst	Lemongrass Sandalwood Lemon Clary sage
The Crown Chakra	Moonstone Amethyst Clear Quartz	Lime Cedarwood Helichrysum Rose Lavender

PART THREE

HEALING WITH ACUPUNCTURE

CHAPTER 7

UNVEILING ACUPUNCTURE

Acupuncture has a long history that dates back thousands of years. Yet, despite this, there are still many who question this method of healing. People want to know exactly how small needles poked into our bodies can heal us physically and mentally. This healing method may sound unempirical, but it has proven its effectiveness repeatedly.

What Is Acupuncture?

Acupuncture is used to treat a variety of physical and mental problems. It involves inserting tiny needles into the skin at various locations on the body where energy channels known as meridians run. The needles are placed into meridians to release energy blockages, allowing a person's energy to flow freely. This therapy promotes wellbeing and aids in the treatment of certain diseases.

How Acupuncture Works

The body, according to traditional Chinese culture, has a vast network of channels known as meridians. Meridians are the pathways that enable energy to run through the body. They lead to important organs in our bodies via the head, hands, and feet. Acupuncture stimulates specific points in the meridians, allowing blocked energy to flow freely through the body, healing ailments and reducing discomfort.

Acupuncturists are experts in the comprehensive study of the meridians. It's part of their anatomy. There are twelve meridians, and each one has a distinct yin and yang aspect. This is what distinguishes the flow of energy. When a person is healthy, their yin and yang energy forces are balanced and harmonised. However, the body becomes ill when the two forces are out of balance and do not work in harmony. As a result, the body is vulnerable to various diseases, both mental and physical. Acupuncture's basic premise is to rebalance the two energies, enabling free passage of energy for the body to recover.

Acupuncture and Your Health

Acupuncture has been around for over two thousand years. It's used to treat various health issues, with evidence to prove that it's a great alternative to Western medicine.

Below are the medical treatments it has been known to cure over the years.

- Anxiety
- Depression
- Chronic pains (these are common to the neck, head, knees, and back)
- Hypertension
- Insomnia
- Allergies
- Osteoarthritis

- Menstrual cramps
- Sprains
- Strokes
- Morning sickness

CHAKRA ACUPUNCTURE

When acupuncture is used for energy healing, it is referred to as "Chakra acupuncture." This healing procedure combines our energy flow and acupuncture to stimulate deep chakra balancing, eliminating negative energy and blockages inside the meridians. Chakra acupuncture unites ancient Chinese energy healing expertise with the Indian notion of the chakra system.

In traditional Chinese culture, qi is a vital force believed to be present in all living things. Qi can imply "material energy," "life force," or "energy flow", in addition to "air." In Chinese medicine and martial arts, it is one of the most fundamental concepts. Acupuncture helps by clearing blockages and stagnation that prevent Qi from flowing freely and balanced. We would have stronger immunity and physiological and psychological well-being if we could acquire vitality through the harmonious flow of Qi. As a result, some health problems like insomnia, tension, headaches, and bodily aches would disappear.

This therapy uses acupuncture at pressure points in the body near the chakras to promote harmony between the chakras and meridians. Activating the chakras releases any blockages of energy within them; stimulating these points with acupuncture is known as the "opening of the chakras." As a result, the energy that flows through the chakras and meridians is balanced and harmonised.

Chakra acupuncture helps with various mental and physical ailments. In addition, this treatment is beneficial for those who are experiencing:

Low energy and lack of strength

Emotional imbalance, which may come in the form of overactive, or suppressed emotions.

Holding on to past trauma or shock.

Stress and anxiety.

The need to achieve calmness and peace.

The need to reconnect with inner balance.

The need to restore energy systems.

Acupuncture has a profound link with your energy. It works well with balancing chakras, which assists in living a balanced and satisfying life, regardless of your mental or physical needs.

PART FOUR

AYURVEDIC THERAPY

CHAPTER 8

HEALING WITH AYURVEDA

Ayurveda is considered one of the oldest holistic healing therapies. Originating over 5000 years ago in India. It's often referred to as the mother of all healing, although the term Ayurveda means "the science of life". Ayurvedic therapy is about the prevention of illness rather than a cure. It promotes optimal health and energy flow through the mind, diet, lifestyle, and use of natural roots, herbs, and minerals.

Ayurveda and the Elements

The basic premise of Ayurveda is that everything in existence, which includes humans, comes from five elements, or what is called basic building blocks. These elements are:

Fire: The principle of radiance

Water: The principle of cohesion

Earth: The principle of inertia

Air: The principle of vibration

Ether: The principle of the pervasiveness

Ayurveda recognises three primary forms of energy in all living things: Vata, Pitta, and Kapha, which are referred to as Doshas and produced by combining the five elements of fire, water, earth, air, and ether. This is the constitution that has a significant impact on our health and wellbeing. The Doshas also have an impact on our behaviour and personality.

The Doshas

Vata = Ether + Air: The energy of this Dosha is movement. It's formed by the combination of air and ether. It's light, dry, cold, moves quickly, rough, and changeable. Vata people are lively and enthusiastic, proficient, and have financial fluidity. They are slim in build and have angular features. When their Vata is balanced, they are creative and social. However, suppose there is an imbalance in their Vata. In that case, they tend to suffer nervous disorders such as anxiety and will experience erratic digestion.

Pitta = Fire + Water: This is the energy of digestion and metabolism. This Dosha is formed by combining fire and water. It's hot, intense, light, spicy, acidic, and sharp. It controls digestion, energy production, and metabolism. Pitta people find it easy to build their muscles, and their complexion is bright. They also have a piercing gaze. Naturally, they are fiery. When this element is balanced, Pitta people will be contented and be clear-minded. They function well as leaders and have strong organisational tendencies. However, if the Pitta is unbalanced, they want to dominate, are quick to anger, and often engage in arguments;. They tend to suffer from excessive body heat, heartburn, acne, and indigestion. They are more susceptible to heart disease or high blood pressure.

Kapha = Earth and Water: This Dosha is formed by the combination of Earth and water. It is heavy, steady, slow, cold, oily, soft, and solid. Kapha people are steady in nature and have a strong build, yet they are generally sweet, loving, and loyal.

When this element is balanced, a Kapha person is forgiving, steady, generous, serene, calm, loving, loyal, supportive, patient, and courageous. But when it is out of balance, a Kapha person can suffer from fluid retention, depression, lethargy, resistance to change, allergies, and weight gain.

Ayurveda states that our Prakriti is the Dosha balance that we have from birth. Therefore, to enjoy optimal health, we should try to support our Prakriti and create harmony among the Doshas in our bodies. This harmony can be created through our diet and our lifestyle modification because the imbalance can manifest as an ailment or disease. Ayurveda refers to two essential concepts that are the keys to achieving holistic wellness. These concepts are Agni and Prana.

Agni: This is our digestive "fire." An Ayurvedic lifestyle aims to stoke our furnace and fuel our digestive fire to efficiently digest our food. We must do this to get full nourishment and nutrients from the food we eat. In addition, it can release all waste products completely to ensure that our bodies accumulate fewer toxins.

Prana: This is the fundamental human life force energy that permeates all living things. Ayurveda seeks to optimise this energy through our lifestyle and nutrition by focusing on the Heart, warmth, and natural foods. It also proposes a daily schedule that is in sync with our bodies' inherent rhythms.

Ayurvedic Treatments

Ayurvedic therapies are used to cleanse the body of pollutants and restore balance as part of the purification process. Below is a list of Ayurvedic treatments, along with a brief description of what each therapy involves.

Treatments performed in Ayurveda.

Abhyanga: This treatment uses warm oils containing healing substances. Each oil is assigned to each Dosha and applied to parts of the body, leaving the skin soft and hydrated. These oils penetrate far below the surface of the skin, which encourages circulation in the body.

Shirodhara: An oil containing herbs is poured across the forehead in what is considered the greatest Ayurvedic technique. Some of the recipes used in this treatment date back more than 2000 years. The head is then massaged with a continuous oil flow, which is claimed to relieve stress, nervous tension and promote relaxation.

Netra Basti: According to Ayurvedic beliefs, the eyes are related to the Sun. The entire eye socket is bathed in warmed butter/oils known as ghee. It originated in ancient India and is used in traditional medical and religious beliefs.

Pinda Sveda: This is a form of massage performed with heated cotton bags packed with various herbs. Through the heat of the cotton bags, this therapy promotes joint relaxation and tension release.

Ayurvedic herbal baths: A bath prepared with flowers, herbs, and oils. Used to soothe muscles and relax the body.

Shiro abhyanga: This is a head massage performed lying down or in a seated position.

Shirovasti: The most intensive and powerful external oil application. Shirovasti is a unique technique for applying medicinal oil to the head. First, the client is seated upright on a stool. The head is then fitted with a cap made of flexible leather that is open on both sides. Finally, the recommended warm, medicinal oil is poured over the cap.

Ayurveda wraps Various wraps and scrubs formulated with natural ingredients, herbs, and oils, to correspond with your body type.

Ayurvedic masks: Like western formulated face masks, healing clays, herbs and oils, and other natural ingredients like algae are used to soothe, revitalise, rejuvenate, and detoxify the skin

The Ayurvedic Diet

According to Ayurvedic medicine principles, the meals we eat should be based on our Ayurvedic body type. An Ayurvedic diet detects your dominant Dosha and encourages you to eat foods proven to heal it, thereby balancing all three doshas. For all three doshas, red meat, artificial sweeteners, and processed components should be avoided; instead, eat healthy whole foods.

In comparison to the Western method, Ayurveda approaches diet from a distinct perspective. Carbohydrates, proteins, fruits, and vegetables are typically emphasised in the Western diet. On the other hand, Ayurveda promotes whole foods and views food through the six tastes of sweet, salty, sour, bitter, spicy, and astringent.

An Ayurvedic diet determines your dominant Dosha and encourages eating foods that will balance all three doshas. Below are dietary considerations relating to each Dosha.

Vata Dietary Recommendations

• They are drawn to raw foods such as vegetables and salads, but their diet is balanced with warm, cooked dishes and sweet, sour, and salty flavours.

• Cold weather, cold beverages, and cold foods can cause unbalance.

• Respond well to foods that are warm, moist, slightly oily, and heavy.

• Three to four small meals every day.

• Snack throughout the day to keep a 2-hour interval between meals.

• Establishing a routine for mealtimes is essential.

• While limiting raw foods aids digestion, a salad with an oil dressing will satisfy a Vata.

• Sweet, ripe, and juicy fruits work well; avoid drying fruits such as apples, cranberries, and pomegranates.

• Fruit should be consumed alone on an empty stomach.

• Legumes are difficult to digest; if you want to eat them, choose the split variety and soak in water overnight before cooking.

Vata balancing general guidelines:

• Stay warm by avoiding the chilly weather and cold foods.

• Remain calm.

• Stick to a routine that includes plenty of rest.

Pitta Dietary Recommendations

• Eat cool, revitalising meals.

• Avoid spicy, sour, and salty foods, as well as foods with a strong smell.

• Vegetarian diets are frequently used to balance Pitta.

• Pitta actively supports raw vegetables and salads.

• Sour fruits should be avoided, though limes can be used sparingly

• Legumes, particularly black lentils, chickpeas, and mung beans, are best; the rest should be eaten in moderation

• Limit spices, nuts, and seeds

• Sweet dairy products are good to include in the diet

• Coffee, alcohol, and tobacco should be avoided.

Pitta balancing general guidelines:

• Avoid excessive heat; limit salt consumption; consume cooling, non-spicy meals; and exercise later in the day, when temperatures are cooler.

Kapha Dietary Recommendations

• Most balanced by bitter, strong-smelling foods but attracted to sweeter, salty, oily foods.

• Use only honey as a sweetener.

• Avoid dairy products and fats, especially those that are high in saturated fat.

• They should consume fewer grains and beans.

• While all vegetables are beneficial for Kapha balance, sweet-sour or juicy vegetables should be avoided.

• Steamed or stir-fried vegetables are easier to digest, while raw vegetables can still be eaten.

• Apples, apricots, mangos, peaches, and pears should be included in the diet.

• Limit heavy foods such as nuts, seeds, and oils.

• Spices, particularly ginger and garlic, can be included in the diet, except for salt.

• Coffee and tea may be drunk occasionally.

Kapha balancing general guidelines:

• Avoid heavy, fatty, oily foods and dairy.

• Maintain your activity level by engaging in frequent physical activity.

• Eat light dry food

Using Ayurveda for Optimal Well-being

Ayurveda understands the truth: there is a natural vibrational rhythm within us all and the Universe. The Doshas, "Vata, Pitta, and Kapha", are energetic forces that govern our life. If we understand these forces, we can tune into the universal vibration and live an abundant, harmonious life. In 24hr, there are three cycles in the day and three at night. Every four hours is dominated by one of the doshas and the qualities that Dosha has. Every cycle combines two out of the five elements: air, fire, water, earth, and ether. Let us look at each cycle.

6:00 a.m. – 10:00 a.m.: Kapha (combines water and Earth)

You may feel a bit slow at this period of the day, and your digestive fire will be lower, especially if you have eaten late at night. This Kapha time is essential for light exercise and to ignite metabolism.

10:00 a.m. – 2:00 p.m.: Pitta (combines fire and water)

At this period, the digestive fire reaches its peak. This is the best time to eat more food. This is also the time you are most productive.

2:00 p.m. – 6:00 p.m.: Vata (combines ether and air)

The body becomes light, and the mind is clear at this time of day. It's the best time for engaging in creativity.

6:00 p.m. – 10:00 p.m.: Kapha (combines water and Earth)

This is the time of the day when the body wants to unwind from everything done in the day. In the late-night, your body will be heavy and tired. Naturally, this is the ideal time to sleep.

10:00 p.m. – 2:00 a.m.: Pitta (combines fire and water)

This is when your evening meal digests. Your thoughts, feelings, and experiences from throughout the day are also digested.

2:00 a.m. – 6:00 a.m.: Vata (combines ether and air)

During this time, sweet dreams occur. You will notice some imbalances in your body, such as waking up to turn or use the bathroom. Waking up at 6a.m. is a terrific way to begin your new day.

The Ayurvedic way of life can help you understand who you are. It will assist you through life by encouraging you to embrace rather than reject your true nature. You may decide to make dietary and lifestyle adjustments to attain a degree of serenity that you have never known before. When you have a sense of balance in your life, you will feel more grounded and energised. Your self-assurance will arise from a deep sense of wellbeing. Ayurvedic knowledge will sustain you in a state of balance, harmony, and contentment.

CHAPTER 9

HEALING CHAKRAS WITH AYURVEDA

The Doshas are linked to the seven major chakras. Understanding this link allows us to perceive the connections between our energetic, subtle, and physical bodies. There are five sub-doshas for each Dosha. These sub-doshas are found in the portions of our bodies governed by the Doshas: Vata, Pitta, and Kapha. When we look at these sub-doshas, we can see the connection to chakras. This is because our physical body influences our energetic body, which is where our chakras are located. In turn, the energetic body has an impact on our mental and emotional wellness.

The Chakras and Sub-Doshas

To understand how the relationship between the Doshas and the Chakras is established, we must first understand the fifteen sub-doshas. Of course, we don't need to know everything there is to know about them. Still, we need to understand the most essential sub-doshas and their relation to the physical and energetic bodies.

The Root Chakra /Muladhara

Vata oversees everything that moves, transports, and communicates in the body. Vata governs the colon and its vitality. The principal function of the colon is to eliminate waste from the human body.

Apana Vata is the sub-dosha that influences colon energy. The energy of the root chakra is governed by this sub-dosha. When there is a problem with elimination, the Apana Vata and root chakras should be healed.

Herbal therapies that aid with elimination are among the healing strategies that work well for Apana Vata and the root chakra. Triphala and Ayurvedic massage treatment are two examples of these therapies. In addition, essential oils such as sweet orange and sweet fennel can also be beneficial.

The Sacral chakra/Svadhistana

The Sacral Chakra is found in the pelvic area. Svadhishthana has the energy of this Chakra and interacts with the Kapha Dosha. This Dosha manages strength, immunity, and stability. The second sub-dosha that works with the Sacral Chakra is Avalambak Kapha. This sub-dosha oversees the energy in the lower back and pelvis. When unbalanced, we can lack emotional, physical, and financial support; we're also more likely to suffer from lower back pain.

Tai chi and other movement therapies, such as dancing, can be beneficial in healing the Sacral Chakra. Also, consider using oil to massage your skin and practising emotional release techniques.

The Solar Plexus Chakra/Manipura

The solar plexus chakra is associated with the Pitta Dosha. This Dosha resonates with transformation, digestion, and metabolism. In addition, it has a sub-dosha called Ranjaka Pitta, which corresponds to the energy of the liver. In Ayurvedic practice, the liver's energy, like the third Chakra, can become "heated" when a person suppresses anger or emotions.

Deep relaxation techniques are used to heal the solar plexus chakra and Ranjaka Pitta. In addition, the use of essential oils and exercises such as martial arts are also extremely beneficial.

The Heart Chakra/Anahata

The heart chakra is also associated with Pitta Dosha energy. Sadhaka Pitta is the sub-dosha associated with the energy of the heart chakra. This is responsible for the fire that fuels our passion. However, this sub-dosha gets imbalanced when we feel mild unhappiness or cannot identify our life's true calling.

A heart-based meditation and oil massage at the heart centre can help heal the fourth Chakra and these sub-dosha imbalances. Essential oils, such as sandalwood oil and rose oil, can also be beneficial.

The Throat Chakra/Vishuddha

The energy of Udana Vata complements the fifth Chakra, which is the throat Chakra. This is the wind that influences our speaking, breathing, and throat. An imbalance with this energy will result in mumbling, stuttering, and throat problems.

To heal the fifth Chakra and its corresponding sub-dosha, you can chant mantras, sing songs or kirtan, and use Nasya essential oil.

The Third Eye Chakra/Anja

The Alochaka Pitta energy is related to our sixth Chakra, positioned in our forehead's centre. The Alochaka Pitta energy governs our eyes and vision. When this energy is out of balance, it causes visual problems and difficulty thinking logically and staying focused.

Shirodhara (pouring oil on the forehead), colouring, and mandalas treat the sixth Chakra and the Alochaka Pitta.

The Crown Chakra/Sahasrara

The energy of Prana Vata is associated with our seventh main Chakra. This sub-dosha oversees the nervous system. When this energy centre is unbalanced, you may find yourself rigid in your beliefs and cannot learn easily from experience. You can heal the crown chakra by meditating or using aromatherapy. Lavender, Lime, Cedarwood,

Helichrysum, and Rose oils are excellent choices. Shirodhara can also be used to heal the crown chakra.

Living a healthy and vibrant life demands more than just a physically good body. We may be physically healthy, but it does not imply that we enjoy a truly healthy life. For example, if you suffer from depression and anxiety, your health is not in decent shape. Using essential oils, crystals, and Ayurvedic practice with your chakras will help you achieve your desired health. True health is multifaceted. It corresponds with our emotional, bodily, and spiritual well-being. The chakras in you are the key window through which you can access your physiological balance, as well as the conduit through which you can understand your life's journey on Earth.

CONCLUSION

Natural resources for self-healing have been bestowed on us all. But if we don't use them, we'll never be able to take advantage of what they have to offer. This book's purpose is to provide you with the knowledge needed to safely and confidently incorporate essential oils into your daily routine for your own health and wellbeing benefits.

I would like to express my gratitude to you for accompanying me on this healing journey so far.

I hope you have enjoyed this book and will follow me to Energy Healing Exploring Mindfulness, the final book in this three-part series.

REFERENCES

n.d. The Essential Life.

2008. Milady's Standard Esthetics. Milady Pub Corp.

Hurst, K., 2020. 7 Chakras: What Is a Chakra? How To Balance Chakras for Beginners. [online] The law of attraction at: https://www.thelawofattraction.com/7-chakras/

Ayurveda: A Brief Introduction and online guide. Available at: www.ayurveda.com/resources/articles/ayurveda-a-brief-introduction-and-guide

Printed in Great Britain
by Amazon